BOOK 3

# THE MANUAL

## SON/SEE/SURF

**CARL BEECH** WITH
ANDY COZENS
AND BEN GRIFFITHS

# BIOGS

## Carl

Carl is married to Karen and has two daughters. He's the leader of CVM (an international men's movement) and the founder of 'the code'. Previously a banker, church planter and senior pastor, he is convinced he is a great chef, plays the piano, loves cycling, movies and sci-fi books and caught a record-breaking catfish on the river Ebro in Spain.
**Twitter** @carlfbeech

## Andy

Andy is 18 years old and, following his A Levels, is working as an intern at CVM. He has a passion for film making and an even bigger passion for Jesus. Andy plans to go to Bible college, and is sure that whatever he goes on to do after that, God will be at the centre and will get the glory. And if it involves film making and telling people about Jesus, all the better!

## Ben

Ben is married to Clare and has two boys. Having been a pro drummer and percussion teacher for 14 years, including a stint as the fastest drummer in the UK, Ben now finds himself in the final throws of vicar training. He likes badminton, pool, movies and cycling with his kids.

Copyright © Carl Beech 2012
Published 2012 by CWR, Waverley Abbey House, Waverley Lane, Farnham, Surrey GU9 8EP, UK.
Registered Charity No. 294387. Registered Limited Company No. 1990308.
The rights of Carl Beech, Andy Cozens and Ben Griffiths to be identified as the authors of this work has been asserted by them in accordance with the Copyright, Designs and Patents Act 1988.

For a list of National Distributors visit www.cwr.org.uk/distributors
Unless otherwise indicated, all Scripture references are from the Holy Bible: New International Version (NIV), copyright © 1973, 1978, 1984, 2011 by Biblica (formerly the International Bible Society).
Concept development, editing, design and production by CWR
Printed in Croatia by Zrinski
ISBN: 978-1-85345-883-5

BOOK 3

# Contents

Introduction
01  A Cheeky Bit of James
08  The End is in Sight
13  Blessed
24  Give Over Andy Cozens
28  A Quick Blast of John
29  On Leading a New Life
33  Surf a Psalm
36  Know Your Place
38  Good Relations
44  Choose Life! Ben Griffiths
48  Internal Workings

**We've finally cracked it!**
After being asked to write daily notes for men a number of times over the years, we've finally nailed it. So, in a nutshell, here you go and let the journey begin!

It's a simple and well-proven approach. The notes are between 150–300 words long. Each day begins with a verse and ends in a prayer. It will take you no more than a few minutes to read but I hope that what you read stays in your head throughout your day. The notes are numbered rather than dated, so it's OK if you miss a day to pick it back up. If you want to study with a group of guys you can easily keep track of where you are up to or swap ideas on that particular study online (we've a Facebook page). If you want to be part of a band of brothers internationally swapping thoughts, insights and prayer requests then you can do that as well by using our new Facebook page.

In each issue, I've asked some of my mates to contribute. In this one, big thanks go to Andy Cozens and Ben Griffiths for their insights and thoughts. They're both great guys going after God's heart. We really hope that the subjects from Son to Surf really speak into all our lives and help us stay on the narrow path.

So there it is. The Word of God has such power to inform and transform our lives, so let's knuckle down and get reading.

Your brother in Christ
**Carl**

# [A CHEEKY BIT OF JAMES]

## 01/Zero in

'But when you ask, you must believe and not doubt, because the one who doubts is like a wave of the sea, blown and tossed by the wind.' **James 1:6**

Powerful stuff, this – but it can be either life-giving or toxic. When we look at a verse in isolation like this, we need to be careful how we apply it. James isn't talking here about asking for a hot tub or a Caterham sports car and getting it, just because you're convinced that you need it; he's talking about asking for wisdom. It's plain and simple, really. Ask for wisdom, it says in verse 5, and according to verse 6 you will get it. You just need to believe and not doubt.

I think that's pretty insightful stuff. If you're in a situation where you really need wisdom, usually it means you're under pressure and finding it hard to know which way to go with a decision. So, get focused, ask for help, then zero in on the problem and make a decision trusting that God is with you.

Simple! Let me tell you, there have been a number of times over the years when I've really not known how to approach a particular situation or which way to turn. It has only been after praying and seeking God in the matter that I've suddenly sensed a real clarity as to the way forward.

Just a caveat here. Usually the best decisions are made with the aid not just of prayer but reading the Bible regularly and surrounding yourself with good people who have wise things to say to you.

---

**Prayer: Father, please grant me wisdom today and whenever I find myself in a situation where I need to make a sharp decision. I believe, I don't doubt, that in those times You will hear my prayer and help me. Amen.**

---

# 02/ Listen up and crack on!

'Anyone who listens to the word but does not do what it says is like someone who looks at his face in a mirror and, after looking at himself, goes away and immediately forgets what he looks like.' **James 1:23-24**

Another way of putting it is 'He's all talk and no action' or 'all foam, no beer'. I could go on.

There's nothing in the world worse than someone who has all the words, all the knowledge, all the bluster but essentially does absolutely nothing about it. I've met blokes like this over the years. Talk about a big cycle ride over a mountain and they will wax lyrical about the climb, only for you to discover that they haven't been on a bike since the Boer War. You see it all the time in male culture. Put bluntly, James has no time for this here. To him it's as ridiculous as forgetting what you look like.

The solution is simple. Every now and again, us men should carry out an internal MOT which checks our Are-we-cracking-on-with-living-the-gospel? factor. Ask ourselves questions like: When was the last time we told someone about Jesus? Are we known for being generous, patient and kind? Otherwise, we'll get a reputation for being all mouth and no trousers – and that's not a good look! Read the Word – and then do it.

---

**Prayer: Help me to be a doer of the Word and not just some bloke who has all the knowledge but doesn't do anything about it. Protect me from being empty of actions but full of talk. Amen.**

---

# 03/Shut it!

'Those who consider themselves religious and yet do not keep a tight rein on their tongues deceive themselves, and their religion is worthless.' **James 1:26**

There are many angles to consider here. There are the guys who say they are followers of Jesus but swear on the footy pitch or in the pub. We need to be careful and guard our distinctiveness – men pick up on these things. Then there are the guys who have nothing positive to say – it's all criticism and complaining. Worse still are the blokes who snipe and moan and pull down their brothers behind their backs. That's friendly fire of the worst kind.

What comes out of our mouths has the ability to build up someone or something hugely or to destroy them. The old saying 'Words will never hurt me' is a load of rubbish, really. Words can have a devastating impact when said with venom. So, my simple advice is this: If you have nothing positive to say (and that can include constructive criticism) and if you lack the ability to give the benefit of the doubt and believe the best, it's wiser to say nothing at all.

Also, going back to my first point, if you find that your words are a little less than pure, ask God to help you tame your tongue. The words you speak are almost impossible to take back once they've been said. That's why James is so blunt here – there's a lot at stake!

---

**Prayer: May the words that come from my lips reflect You, Father, and Your heart. Purify my thoughts so that increasingly what I say is clean and fault-free. Amen.**

---

# 04/Doing stuff

'What good is it, my brothers and sisters, if someone claims to have faith but has no deeds? Can such faith save them? Suppose a brother or a sister is without clothes and daily food. If one of you says to them, "Go in peace; keep warm and well fed," but does nothing about their physical needs, what good is it? In the same way, faith by itself, if it is not accompanied by action, is dead.' **James 2:14-17**

I know a guy who was totally transformed by the message of Jesus. According to him, it was like walking out of a black-and-white picture into a high-definition, Technicolor picture with all the trimmings! For many of us, this then means just going to church, joining in with all the stuff that goes on there and trying to get our heads round the Bible and share our faith. My mate took it a step further, however. Compelled by these verses, he ended up giving 50% of his income away and founding a work in Africa among some of its poorest people.

We can't all do that, of course, but I am convinced that meeting Jesus compels us to do stuff as well as believe stuff. I don't think we can ignore the Third World in our giving. We also can't ignore the needs on our own doorsteps. To follow Jesus is more than just Sunday faith and saying the right things. It also means getting our hands dirty and giving our time, skills and heart to those who have less than us. Perhaps we should ask God where we can be used for His kingdom to make a difference to the lives around us. I think that's a prayer He answers very quickly.

---

**Prayer: Show me where the needs are and help me to get stuck into meeting them. I commit whatever skills, time and money I have available to help fix a broken world and meet people's needs. Amen.**

---

# 05/Fight the greed!

'What causes fights and quarrels among you? Don't they come from your desires that battle within you? You desire but do not have, so you kill. You covet but you cannot get what you want, so you quarrel and fight. You do not have because you do not ask God. When you ask, you do not receive, because you ask with wrong motives, that you may spend what you get on your pleasures.' **James 4:1-3**

One of my mates used to joke about being covetous. Whenever he saw someone he knew with a better car than him, or a slinky new piece of gadgetry, he would say, 'There's only one cure for coveting. Buy it!'

Now, obviously he was joking but it does point to a serious human condition. It's true to say that once you get caught in a spiral of coveting stuff and then buying it, the law of diminishing returns sets in. When that happens, it's always going to take the next bigger and better thing to make you happy – and that's a road to a lot of pain! More than that, what James is saying here is that it's those desires battling within you that cause you to start falling out with other people. Then you start praying for things that aren't after God's heart and you lose perspective. That's how someone in the wealthy West can pray for a new Mercedes while someone in Somalia is praying for rain so that his family can eat.

Better to enjoy the simple things and live a life of gratitude for what we have.

---

**Prayer: Protect me from greed and help me to set my heart on what You want for me and not on what other people have. Help me to be grateful and enjoy the simple things. Amen.**

---

# 06/Stand your ground!

'Submit yourselves, then, to God. Resist the devil, and he will flee from you.' **James 4:7**

What does it mean to submit to God? Well, I guess it means, first of all, that you have to know what God wants. And you get to know what God wants by staying close to Him, using the age-old methods of reading the Bible, praying and hanging out with other guys who are also trying to follow Him. The plain and simple truth is that the enemy is a sharpshooter and he's looking for guys he can pick off because they've become isolated and exposed. When Jesus stood His ground in the desert, He used the Word of God (our only offensive weapon, according to Ephesians 6). Shortly after this skirmish the devil left, because he couldn't stand up to it.

How about this for a kind of routine for holding the line? When you get up in the morning, at some point – maybe as you haul yourself out of the sack or find yourself having a shave or a quiet cuppa – commit the day, your plans and your life to God. Use these notes to get some focus and try to remember the verses we've been reading. Resolve to use your life for God this day. He will draw close to you as a result and the enemy will find it hard to take you out.

---

**Prayer: I commit my day, my plans, my thoughts and my actions to You, God. I will walk with You step by step and in company with those around me who also follow You. Amen.**

---

We gain the strength of the temptation we resist.
**RALPH WALDO EMERSON**

# 07/Just wait!

'Be patient, then, brothers and sisters, until the Lord's coming. See how the farmer waits for the land to yield its valuable crop, patiently waiting for the autumn and spring rains. You too, be patient and stand firm, because the Lord's coming is near.' **James 5:7-8**

We've probably all been there. Something goes wrong and we throw a sort of mild sulking fit which has the subtext: Where was God when I needed Him? Why didn't He answer me when I prayed?

In fact, one of the most familiar cries from the hearts of Christian blokes is that in the tough times, when the chips are down, God doesn't seem to respond. It's at such times that we need to recall verses like these. The guys who wrote the Bible were no strangers to tough times or the sense that God didn't seem to be answering them. Of course, it's only with the benefit of hindsight that we see that He was in the situation after all.

So, in times like that, stand firm, hold the line, keep praying and keep looking up! That's why we need to base our faith on more than feelings. We need to ground it in the truth about God's character and a knowledge of the story the Bible tells over thousands of years of a God who stays true to His promises and cannot lie.

In the end, things will all work out for good. So, be patient and remember that one day the Lord will return. That's what the Bible says and I'm sticking to the party line!

---

**Prayer: Help me to hold the line, not just when times are good but when they are tough as well. Grant me patience and a steady spirit. Protect me from being volatile, a man whose faith is strong only when times are good. Amen.**

---

# [THE END IS IN SIGHT]

## 08/No excuses

'His divine power has given us everything we need for a godly life through our knowledge of him who called us by his own glory and goodness.' **2 Peter 1:3**

So, we have everything we need for a godly life? More than that, in fact - it is through God's divine power that we have all we need to live it. Seems too good to be true? Well, if the Bible says it, I believe it. However, we need to take a second look. It says here that this comes chiefly through our knowledge of God. I really do think that's key. The issue for many of us is that life can be so busy that we squeeze out the very thing we need to do if we want to not just survive but thrive: getting to know God in increasing depth.

Those of us who are married will know that for a marriage to do more than limp along - or fail - you need to spend time together. This isn't rocket science, but it's amazing how many of us get it wrong. The weeks and months fly past in a flurry of activity and, being blokes, we just keep our heads down and crack on. Then, you stop and look around you and realise that you're losing ground in your relationship with your wife and/or kids. (Those of you who aren't married, still take note – it applies to other relationships too!)

It's the same with the way we practise our faith. Yes, we have divine power to help us but in reality we find that it's not there because we're failing to engage with God in enough depth. Take the time to get to know Him better and you will be all the stronger for it. That's a fact straight from the Bible.

---

**Prayer: Show me Your ways, God, and help me to learn more about You so that I can stand strong as I draw that strength from You. Amen.**

---

# 09/Weird stuff

'But there were also false prophets among the people, just as there will be false teachers among you. They will secretly introduce destructive heresies, even denying the sovereign Lord who bought them – bringing swift destruction on themselves.' **2 Peter 2:1**

At the time when this was written, the Early Church was under siege from people claiming special new insights and revelations about Jesus, and all kinds of weird distortions of the Christian faith. Nothing new there, then. We're always going to have people around us who think they know better than the Bible and we're always going to need to be on our guard against people (including leaders) who claim to have a new insight that's gone undiscovered since the time of Jesus. In our culture, we have a love for sensational claims and our ears itch for the latest new thing. That's OK if they're true but more often than not the simple reality is that we haven't got the stuff that's written down in the Bible right, let alone any new stuff. I could give you so many examples of strange things people have told me are of God that have turned out to be anything but.

So, if someone comes along with a new insight that guarantees you more money, better looks, more healing power and an altogether better life, I personally would run a mile. Jesus tells us how to get life to the full. For starters, the Beatitudes give us a pretty countercultural way to live – and they're hard enough without anything else being added!

So, keep it simple and keep your radar on!

---

**Prayer: Help me to stay on the narrow path and to be obedient to Your Word. Protect my heart and mind from false claims and heresy. Strengthen me to challenge those who come claiming to have new teaching, which only takes others away from the truth. Amen.**

---

# 10/On your guard

'But the day of the Lord will come like a thief. The heavens will disappear with a roar; the elements will be destroyed by fire, and the earth and everything done in it will be laid bare.' **2 Peter 3:10**

A few years ago, there was a break-in at my house. It was the strangest thing, really. They got into my garage and took my fishing kit and motorcycle gear. It was pretty surreal. I went out and everything was there; I came back and a load of stuff was gone! They hadn't disturbed anything else – it was as if a bunch of my possessions had just vanished into thin air. Most disturbing was the fact that they had left my motorbike behind! OK, it was an old heap, but that was just plain insulting ...

So it will be, the Bible says, when Jesus comes back. It will be as if a stealthy thief has come and we will be taken totally by surprise. Because of this, we ought to protect ourselves from getting distracted and losing ground. We ought to live as if the return of Jesus is imminent and not thousands of years away. The Early Church lived with that perspective, which fuelled its mission and its behaviour.

OK, so take it to the extreme and we stop living life to the full. I get that. It's a balance, though, isn't it? We should live the lives God has given us to live but also bear in mind, somehow, that this present life is not the full story and will come to an end. That's a tough balance to maintain, but I think it's a tension we ought to try and live with more.

---

**Prayer: I don't want to be caught off guard, nor do I want to live in fear that I'm losing focus. Help me to keep looking up while also cracking on with the life You have given me. Amen.**

---

# 11/Watch out!

'Since everything will be destroyed in this way, what kind of people ought you to be? You ought to live holy and godly lives as you look forward to the day of God ...' **2 Peter 3:11**

There are many motives for leading what you might call a 'holy' life. Perhaps it's about not dishonouring what Jesus has done for you. Perhaps it's fear of being caught. But how about this one? To paraphrase what Peter says: God's going to destroy the world and start again – and it's going to come out of the blue. So, watch out and hold the line!

Interesting one, that. I can see the point, though. Life ticks along and you get yourself to church or homegroup, you try to read the Bible (though you don't always keep up with it) and every now and again you do something you later regret. Perhaps the years roll past and it seems like God is a bit distant or not as real as He once was. Perhaps your conscience isn't as sharp as it used to be, you're not giving quite as much time and money as you once did and your attitude is more cynical and pessimistic than in times past. If that's you, read this and take note! Keep sharp, because one day the heavens will disappear with a roar. Keep looking up, this verse is saying to us; keep looking up and remember that (as we said yesterday) one day the thief in the night will come and pay a visit to an unsuspecting world.

---

**Prayer: Keep me sharp and focused. Keep my thoughts on track and my actions after Your heart. Keep me ready, as if You were coming back today. Amen.**

---

My home is in heaven. I'm just travelling through this world.
**BILLY GRAHAM**

# 12/Acceleration

'Since everything will be destroyed in this way, what kind of people ought you to be? You ought to live holy and godly lives as you look forward to the day of God and speed its coming. That day will bring about the destruction of the heavens by fire, and the elements will melt in the heat.' **2 Peter 3:11-12**

Today, we focus on verse 12.

So, because the world is going to get wiped out, we ought to live holy and godly lives? That seems a bit strange at first reading. Some blokes might take the fact that everything is going to get done in as an excuse to do literally 'what the hell they want' – following the attitude of Jim Morrison who famously wanted to 'get my kicks' before the whole place went up in flames. The thing is, though, that there is something else buried in these verses, which hints at the influence a life lived for God can have.

What Peter seems to be saying is that if we live for God, we can hasten the end!

That in itself raises all sorts of questions in my head. Do I *want* Jesus to return now? What about my family who don't know him? What about the experiences in this life I've yet to have? The more you look at these two verses, the more questions they stir up – at least, they do for me. The bottom line, though, is to keep our eyes fixed on the King and the coming kingdom, lest we fall short and miss the point. I guess we can content ourselves with the knowledge that God is fair and just and won't let us down.

---

**Prayer: I keep my eyes fixed on King Jesus and the coming of His reign. May I bear Your name with honour, Jesus, and live my life to please You! Amen.**

---

# [BLESSED]

## 13/ He went, they followed

'Now when Jesus saw the crowds, he went up on a mountainside and sat down. His disciples came to him, and he began to teach them.'
**Matthew 5:1-2**

I don't think I'm as good at listening as I should be. Some of that's just the way my brain is wired. If I'm already occupied when you speak to me, I may not notice because I'm so tuned in to what I'm doing. However, sometimes I don't listen because, if I'm honest, I think I know better than everyone else. That's pretty bad, really, and I need to work on it.

I'm inspired by this short verse. I love the way it says the disciples came to Him. Jesus didn't need to shout for attention. Nor did He use fancy methods to attract a crowd. He had something compelling and revolutionary to say and people wanted to hear Him. My question today for us guys is this: Are we listening to Jesus? Are we sitting at His feet? Are we going to Him to learn or do we just go to Him when we want something? Perhaps we need to start practising turning aside for a time to listen and not speak. To read the Bible and not offer comment, just letting it sink in. I think we would be better men for that.

---

**Prayer: Heavenly Father, thank You for Your patience with me and the way You take time to work with me. In return, I determine to take more time to listen to You and not speak, to learn from You and not just make requests. In Jesus' name. Amen.**

---

# 14/Poor in spirit

'Blessed are the poor in spirit, for theirs is the kingdom of heaven.'
**Matthew 5:3**

Let's cut to the chase as we work through the Beatitudes for a bit. First, to be 'blessed' here means more than feeling good about stuff. It means to have *shalom*: to be complete, fully made up, brand new and more. In other words, it's the ultimate place to be!

But what on earth does it mean to be 'poor in spirit'? Obviously, there is loads of stuff out there on this subject. Google it and you'll be overwhelmed by different opinions. I reckon that us men just need to take the verse at face value and get to grips with the fact that knowing our *need* of God is the best way to keep ourselves on the straight and narrow. Being a bit smart (cue Google again), the word for 'poor' here is *ptochos*, which literally means 'folded' and suggests someone who is trying to make themselves small – like someone on the street without a bed for the night, maybe, who is trying to protect themselves from the elements and escape the attention of muggers. The bottom line is that all the money in the world, and the smartest house and flashiest car, won't save us from meeting God one day. When that happens, we'll be stripped of all the trappings. I guess the trappings are just smoke and mirrors anyway.

So, keep it real and remember: anything you have is because of God's grace. Once we get that, we start to see the world differently. We become more generous, more prayerful and more on the case with telling people the message of Jesus. Blessed indeed! In fact, live like that and the kingdom is yours ...

---

**Prayer: I remember today that all I have is because of the grace You have shown me. That being so, I'm determined not to get ahead of myself or think that it's all about me. Help me to stay humble and focused on You. Amen.**

---

# 15/Comforted

'Blessed are those who mourn, for they will be comforted.' **Matthew 5:4**

We mourn for loads of different reasons. The death of someone we were close to. An ongoing situation that causes us grief. Or perhaps our own sense of being messed up in front of God.

I remember when I started to do stuff with my church. I was stepping out for the first time, trying to tell people about Jesus as part of a street team after work. It was in the middle of all that that I suddenly started to become aware that deep inside I was a bit of a doughnut. Worse than that, stuff I was doing when no one was looking, that I had managed to hide away from everyone else and even convince myself was no big deal, started to trouble me. In other words, I became aware that I was a sinner.

It was then that I realised what grace really is. I had a wake-up call that not only did Jesus love me but it was because of this that I could get my head straight and crack on with being the kind of man I knew I ought to be. In other words, I was being comforted. And that, brothers, helped me to press on. Nice one!

So, let's be honest with ourselves and get real about our lives. Where are we in denial about what we are really like? What kind of men are we when no one is looking? Where do we need to get things straight?

---

**Prayer: Whatever is going on in my life right now and whatever lies ahead of me, I know that You are my Comforter. Thank You, God, for Your grace and care. Help me to live my life in a way that responds to this and pleases You. Amen.**

---

# 16/Doormat?

'Blessed are the meek, for they will inherit the earth.' **Matthew 5:5**

A friend of mine who works on the trading floor of an investment bank ripped into his team once for messing something up. It's fair to say that it's a high-pressure place – a testosterone-rich environment where the financial stakes are very high and people don't pull any punches. The potential for losing your rag is huge! That evening, he and I were sitting chatting over a beer and replaying the incident. He told me, 'I don't think I did the Christian cause any favours today. I was out of order in the way I dealt with the problem. I'll do something about it tomorrow.'

And here's what he did. In a place where people don't take any prisoners and apologies are few and far between, he gathered all his team together and asked them for their forgiveness. He told them that he had let them down and that many of them were better and more talented men than him. He told them that it was a privilege to work with them and that he shouldn't have sworn or lost it, even though mistakes had been made. Now, that's meek. Not weak, just humble and grace-filled.

It takes courage to be like that, especially when any admission that you were wrong can have the predators sniffing for blood. Jesus, it seems to me, exercised power by getting nailed to a cross. He didn't do things the way others did – He even forgave those who were crucifying Him. That is the example we follow. The way of Jesus is countercultural. That's why the meek inherit the earth.

---

**Prayer: Please give me the strength to be meek and the courage to walk in humility. Amen.**

---

# 17/Fill me!

'Blessed are those who hunger and thirst for righteousness, for they will be filled.' **Matthew 5:6**

I hunger and thirst for a lot of things but, I confess, not always righteousness. It seems to me that there are a lot of things vying for our attention, and more than a few that distract us from the things of God. So, how on earth do we keep ourselves hungry and thirsty for righteousness? For me, it's all about doing kingdom things: finding opportunities to share my faith, meeting up with mates who hold me to account, being generous, believing the best, reading the Bible etc. Gradually, over time, it puts my focus more on the King and His kingdom.

One thing I used to do, when my Tube train pulled into Oxford Circus each day, was to use the start of the escalators up to ground level to begin a prayer that went something like this: 'Use me today to show You to people and help me to be a man You are pleased with.' It was just a reminder at the start of the day to keep me on track. It worked for me. Have a think about what might work for you. In return, I found that God answered those prayers every day. That's true to His Word, isn't it? Those who seek Him and pursue Him will be filled.

---

**Prayer: Make me a man who pursues righteousness and hungers for the things of Your kingdom. Make me a man who is after Your heart and not one who is derailed by the distractions of this world. Amen.**

---

**[BLESSED]**

# 18/Mercy!

'Blessed are the merciful, for they will be shown mercy.' **Matthew 5:7**

There's a chilling scene in *Schindler's List* where the hero of the film is talking to the commandant of a Nazi concentration camp, a brutal man who likes to stand on his balcony and shoot people for fun. Schindler tries to persuade him that it's a greater display of power to say 'I pardon you' than to put a bullet in someone's head. The commandant tries it for a day or so, but then it's back to the usual horror of random murder.

It's an extreme illustration of a very powerful point. If someone wrongs you, what do you do? Do you lash out in the heat of the moment? Do you take the view that 'revenge is a dish best served cold'? Or do you take the opportunity to practise grace and mercy? After all, God showed us grace by sending His Son to die for us, so why don't we demonstrate grace in return? Instead of harbouring anger or bitterness, why not choose to believe the best of the other person, give them the benefit of the doubt and show them the same grace that you have been shown?

As an aside, it's true to say that you reap what you sow. Everyone is a winner if you go God's way. Is there someone you can call today and make peace with? Is there someone at work you need to clear the decks with? Make it a regular habit, and you'll be a better man for it.

---

**Prayer: Lead me in Your ways and Your understanding. Help me to be known as a gracious and merciful man, not a bitter and vindictive one. Amen.**

---

# 19/Pure

'Blessed are the pure in heart,
for they will see God.' **Matthew 5:8**

Moses was described as the humblest man on the
face of the earth (Num. 12:3) and he saw God face
to face. In fact, we are told that God spoke directly
*only* to Moses (Num. 12:6-8)! So, what does it
mean for us to 'see God'? I think it means that if
we seek Him and keep our hearts pure, we will
see Him at work in and through us.

The thing is, the more I draw close to God, the
more I feel His heart breaking for the world. Years
ago, I was planting a new church on a bust-up
estate that hadn't had any significant investment
for years. The needs behind its (mostly closed)
doors were profound. I was regularly called upon
during the night to deal with guys who were
smashed out of their faces. People were living
lives that were, frankly, wrecked. So many of them
had very little hope, and often I had to confront
situations where people just wanted to give up
on life. One day, I woke up feeling absolutely

broken. In fact, I felt like crying all the time as if I was grief-stricken. Later on that day, I remember a distinct sense of God whispering deep into my heart: 'What you are feeling is how I feel for My people who live here.' It floored me, I can tell you.

So, what does it mean to 'see God'? Perhaps it means not just seeing Him at work but feeling His heart for people as well. Keep your heart pure and you will see God. Just don't expect it to be how you think it will be.

---

**Prayer: Help me to see You at work, help me to feel Your heart. Keep me pure so that I can do Your work. Amen.**

# 20/Peace out!

> 'Blessed are the peacemakers, for they will be called children of God.'
> **Matthew 5:9**

I have a theory about peacemaking: I don't reckon it's a peaceful activity! When Jesus brought peace, He did so at a tremendous cost – and the same is true of so many other peacemakers. Gandhi was assassinated for encouraging Hindus not to resort to violence against Muslims. Martin Luther King was vilified, firebombed, beaten and ultimately murdered. Terry Waite was kidnapped and kept in isolation for years. Yitzhak Rabin was shot dead for signing the Oslo Accords with the Palestinians – I could go on. It seems to me that, in order to make peace, people may have to put themselves in harm's way.

So, what does this mean for your average bloke who isn't a civil-rights campaigner or a UN special envoy? I guess it means standing in the middle of conflict at work. It means brokering peace even if it causes you hassle. It means taking up the cause of the weaker person who doesn't have the ability to stand up for themselves. It means perhaps not ignoring in your prayers (and with your wallet and your time) those in the world who are being attacked or oppressed. Be like this and God will see you as His son.

That's what the Word says, so let's live it! Let's be men who are prepared to take a hit and bear the cost as we stand in the gap and bring peace.

---

**Prayer: Make me a man of peace. Give me the courage and strength I need to place myself in harm's way in order to be a true peacemaker. Amen.**

---

# 21/Under pressure

'Blessed are those who are persecuted because of righteousness, for theirs is the kingdom of heaven.' **Matthew 5:10**

Let's be honest here: there's persecution and there's persecution. It is estimated that every year since 1990 an astonishing 160,000 people worldwide have been killed for being Christians. We should be deeply thankful that we live in a society that leaves us in relative peace.
I believe we should also be making a noise while we can about those in other countries who are losing their lives for their faith*, and we should pray regularly for peace.

That's not to say that we don't face creeping persecution in the West, of course – I just think we need to keep it in perspective. However, if we do face a tough time, from ridicule to blatant opposition, we can be reminded that not only is God there with us in it but the kingdom of heaven is ours.

One other thought occurs to me as I ponder this verse. Just maybe, we don't face much opposition because we are so timid and quiet. I wonder how much more persecution we would experience if we were more upfront. I wonder, too, how vocal or active we would be if the pressure really was upped. Now, there's a challenge!

---

**Prayer: Today I pray for those who are facing torture, imprisonment and death for following Jesus. Grant Your supernatural peace to all those who are suffering because of their faith. Grant grace and strength to those in prison or facing utter injustice. And make me a man of courage and steadfastness so that I will not yield when the pressure comes. Amen.**

---

\*Visit the website of organisations such as Release International, Open Doors and Christian Solidarity Worldwide for more information.

# 22/ Under attack

'Blessed are you when people insult you, persecute you and falsely say all kinds of evil against you because of me. Rejoice and be glad, because great is your reward in heaven, for in the same way they persecuted the prophets who were before you.' **Matthew 5:11-12**

It's tough to stay cool when someone's putting the boot in. I can remember, as a pastor, being summoned to meet a couple of people who were really having a go at me. It seemed there was nothing I was doing right. More than that, they had got completely the wrong end of the stick about a whole range of issues and had approached other people and wound them up a fair bit as well. The end result was a whole bunch of half-truths, misrepresentations and false accusations. I felt stressed and heavy-hearted, to put it mildly.

I'll never forget this, though. As I left for the meeting, Karen, my wife, told me of a song she used to sing in Sunday school: 'With Jesus in the vessel, you can smile at the storm ...' Later, as I sat and faced wave after wave of verbal attacks, that song kept going through my mind. The thing was, I knew that my heart was right and that if I *had* done anything wrong, I could ask my accusers to forgive me – which I did. The upshot was that the truth came out (as it always does in the end) and I kept my head.

The thing is, though, that even if things hadn't been resolved in that meeting, the Bible tells me that one day my reward will be great for doing the right thing. I guess these verses also mean that we are to expect attack for doing God's work. If that wasn't the case, we wouldn't need this encouragement!

---

**Prayer: Help me to keep my head, my peace and my integrity when I'm attacked. Help me to keep my eyes heavenward, even when I'm facing a storm of false accusations. Amen.**

---

# 23/Shine on!

'In the same way, let your light shine before others, that they may see your good deeds and glorify your Father in heaven.' **Matthew 5:16**

This is a bit counter to what we are normally told. Usually, as followers of Jesus we crack on with doing the good stuff in secret, and we don't let our right hand know what our left hand is up to. Here, however, we are told to let people see what we're doing!

There's a reason, though, and it's a good one. Once I was speaking at a conference and a guy came over to me and said: 'I think there's more that you have to say but you don't want to say it in case you look all big and clever. However, bear in mind that if you don't share your stories of what God is doing, you are robbing Him of His glory!' That's so true! We see God doing things in people's lives and we see Him using us but so often we are reluctant to talk about it. I think the onus is basically on us to point beyond ourselves to Jesus and give all the glory to God. The bottom line is this: anything good that people see in us is the result of the work that Someone greater is doing in us! If we can communicate that, then we *should* 'let our lights shine'. How else will people know that God is at work unless we show them?

**Prayer: As I serve You, Lord, and serve Your kingdom, please help me to point beyond myself to Jesus so that my light shines and shows people Your glory, not mine. Amen.**

We should not ask, 'What is wrong with the world?' ... Rather, we should ask, 'What has happened to the salt and light?'
**JOHN R. W. STOTT**

# [GIVE OVER]

## 24/Block it out!

'Do you not know that your bodies are temples of the Holy Spirit, who is in you, whom you have received from God? You are not your own; you were bought at a price. Therefore honour God with your bodies.' **1 Corinthians 6:19-20**

Direct, to the point, no messing around. Paul underlines the fact that our bodies are sacred. Not a shed or a garage – a temple! A dwelling place of the Holy Spirit. Or at least they should be. We are bombarded every day by sexual imagery, but we have a choice to make: Do we let it take root in our thoughts or do we block it out? If we let it take root, we are in danger of defiling our bodies. If we block it out, we remain holy and blameless in God's sight.

But Paul doesn't stop there. He thinks we might need a bit more convincing. That body you're walking around in is not yours and yours alone, but God's. You don't even have the authority to defile your own body! You don't have the excuse 'It's my body, I can do what I like with it!' So, is he saying all this to make us feel guilty? No. He says it so that we may appear holy and blameless in God's sight. He says it so that we can use our bodies for honourable things and not just to please ourselves.

So, when you're being bombarded by sexual imagery, remember that your body is a dwelling place of the Holy Spirit and if you give in to that imagery, you are pinning a centrefold to the front door. Don't let those images in! Learn where your weak points are and ask God to help you board them up, so you can stay free from sexual sin and honour Him with your body.

---

**Prayer: Lord, please show me my weak points and help me to board them up. Help me to use my body to honour You. I don't want to be a slave to sexual sin, I want to be holy and blameless. Amen.**

---

# 25/ Handing over the reins

'Ah, Sovereign LORD, you have made the heavens and the earth by your great power and outstretched arm. Nothing is too hard for you.'
**Jeremiah 32:17**

There are some things in life that us guys like to be in control of – the TV remote, for example. Generally, though, it's the bigger things that we like to keep a grip on, like our career path, where we live or maybe a relationship. It's tough to leave decisions about these kind of things in someone else's hands. But that's exactly what we have to do. We've got to hand the reins over to God.

This can be a daunting prospect sometimes, but (as Jeremiah says here in his prayer) we have a sovereign Father and that means He has ultimate control. By His great power, He made the heavens and the earth. It should be a blessing to us that we can hand our worries over to Him and not resist doing so. He isn't indecisive or foolish, He knows exactly what is best for our lives.

Are you actively seeking God's will in *your* life? Do you trust Him enough to leave those big decisions to Him? Today, if you're holding anything back, whatever it is, if you haven't handed the reins over completely to Him, then ask Him to help you let go.

---

**Prayer: Lord, I give my day over to You now. Any situation I have in my life, big or small, I give to You because I know that nothing is too hard for You. I trust that You know what is best for me and thank You that You are willing to help me. Amen.**

---

# 26/ Planning God out

'Many are the plans in a person's heart, but it is the LORD's purpose that prevails.' **Proverbs 19:21**

Have you ever been responsible for organising a Christian event or programme and packed it full of stuff that you think glorifies God in the best way possible? Too often I've been so focused on filling such things with all my ideas that I've ended up leaving no room for God to do His work. Because I have failed to leave space for God, my plans have not been as effective as I had expected and, in fact, largely failed.

What I have found is that when I leave space for God to work, I see Him move in ways I could never have planned for. Recently, I was involved with a youth mission week and my team leader, Jason, appeared to be very disorganised. He would often leave things until the last minute and generally approached tasks with an 'it'll-be-all-right-on-the-night' attitude. I found this really difficult at first, as I can be quite a perfectionist.

However, I discovered that whenever it seemed like my plans were all going wrong, God was stepping in and working in those situations in His own way, which was generally much better than mine. I came to realise that Jason wasn't being disorganised, he was just leaving space for God.

When God changes your plans, don't get frustrated. They were never yours anyway, they were His.

---

**Prayer: Lord, help me to leave space for You when I am planning to do Your work. Let me conduct myself in a way that does not obstruct Your movement but instead facilitates it. Amen.**

---

# 27/ When I am weak, I'm strong

'He said to me, "My grace is sufficient for you, for my power is made perfect in weakness." Therefore I will boast all the more gladly about my weaknesses, so that Christ's power may rest on me. That is why, for Christ's sake, I delight in weaknesses, in insults, in hardships, in persecutions, in difficulties. For when I am weak, then I am strong.' **2 Corinthians 12:9-10**

For Superman it was Kryptonite, for the Hulk it was his short fuse and for Spider-Man it was Mary Jane. We all have our own Achilles' heel, whether it's pride, road rage, lust, general laziness – the list goes on. We're often made to feel guilt or shame about our weaknesses and so we brush them under the carpet and never face up to them. As a result, either we start to believe the lies the devil speaks to us and condemn ourselves or we deny our weaknesses and they gradually get worse and worse. It's a lose-lose situation.

In this passage, God says that His power is made perfect in weakness. So, how does that work? God does not operate a dictatorship but instead longs for a relationship. However, this can only work if you give everything over to Him. Although God is sovereign, He wants us to choose this path ourselves. When we give everything to Him, He can work at full capacity. Our actions then are not in our own strength but His.

So, the big question is: will you allow God to make you strong?

---

**Prayer: Father, help me today to remember that Your power is made perfect in my weakness. Please help me to focus on Your power as opposed to my own shortcomings. I invite You to work at Your full capacity in every area of my life, for when I am weak, then I am strong. Amen.**

---

## 28/Mentor

'It gave me great joy when some believers came and testified about your faithfulness to the truth, telling how you continue to walk in it.'

`3 John 1:3`

John says it's the business to hear that his 'children' are still walking in the truth. I love that. Here is a guy who has raised up disciples, pointed them towards Jesus, cut them loose to do the stuff and then rejoices when word comes back that they are still on track. I think that each of us guys should be being discipled, and each of us, where possible and appropriate, should be mentoring and discipling younger guys (younger either in years or in the faith). I make it a rule always to have a couple of younger blokes who I invest time in. We pray together, read the Word together, do a bit of life together and basically look to Jesus together. At the same time, I have a few men who are older than me and wiser in the things of God who walk with me.

So, have a think about these important questions today. Who are you investing in? And who is investing in you? I recently went to see the first senior pastor I ever had, the man who raised me into leadership in the church. It was an awesome and precious time. We don't agree on everything – but that's precisely the point. Never stop learning and never put yourself beyond being challenged. You'll be a better man for it.

---

**Prayer: Show me who I should be walking with in this adventure called life, and show me who should be walking with me. I want the experience of hearing one day of men still walking with You who I once invested my time and life in! Amen.**

---

# 29/Dead to sin

'What shall we say, then? Shall we go on sinning, so that grace may increase? By no means! We are those who have died to sin; how can we live in it any longer?'
**Romans 6:1-2**

Quite a few years ago, when I was a student, I went back to the digs of a mate I had met at the Christian Union. Walking into his room was like walking into the red light district in Amsterdam. I couldn't believe it! The walls were absolutely covered in pornographic images. It totally freaked me out – I couldn't quite compute it. How could someone who claimed to be a Christian have that stuff all over his walls? How could he sing to Jesus and wave his arms about like a windmill one minute and then (to be blunt) live with an open sex addiction the next? So, me being me, I decided to ask him about it. The response floored me: 'It's just my issue. It's a sin thing I haven't nailed yet.'

Let me tell you, that's bad news. As soon as you tell yourself that it's just 'your issue', you are heading rapidly into a nightmare scenario. Worse than that, it's almost as if you are pouring scorn on the fact that Jesus got nailed to a lump of wood for your 'sin thing'. And it isn't just porn. What about the bloke with a violent temper who is always losing it, or the guy with the huge bank balance who never thinks of helping the poor? I could go on, but you get the idea.

The Bible is clear. We have died to sin, we don't live in it any longer. Instead, we fight it!

---

**Prayer: May You see in me a pure heart, God. May You see in me a man who doesn't ignore the tough challenges but fights to keep my life right before You. Amen.**

---

# 30/New man

'Don't you know that all of us who were baptised into Christ Jesus were baptised into his death? We were therefore buried with him through baptism into death in order that, just as Christ was raised from the dead through the glory of the Father, we too may live a new life.'
**Romans 6:3-4**

I was baptised when I was 22 and I remember it like it was yesterday. I had this startling feeling as I came up out of the water of the baptistry (basically, a semi-heated half-pint swimming pool) that I was clean. Not clean on the outside, though – clean on the inside. It was a powerful moment. As I went under the water, I remember saying goodbye to the old Carl Beech. I was a new man now and I was going to crack on with giving following Jesus my best shot.

Regardless of your church tradition, the Bible is very clear: at this point in your journey of faith, you die to the old you and are empowered by the Holy Spirit to live a new life. Being by nature a ratbag, I have to keep reminding myself of this. I have to tell myself that there was a day when I died to the old self. It doesn't mean that I'm perfect, of course, or that I don't make mistakes any more. What it means is that I nailed my spiritual colours to the mast and said: 'No going back! I've died to the old me, and now I'm a new man.'

It's good to remind ourselves of that regularly. To remember the day we made our public stand. And if that's something you haven't done yet, then how about it?

---

**Prayer: Thank You, Jesus, that You died for me so that I, too, may live a new life, with a new hope. Help me to be faithful to this and to keep my colours nailed to the mast. Amen.**

---

# 31/ Slave no more

'If we have been united with him like this in his death, we will certainly also be united with him in his resurrection. For we know that our old self was crucified with him so that the body of sin might be done away with, that we should no longer be slaves to sin – because anyone who has died has been freed from sin.' **Romans 6:5-7**

You have the opportunity and the power to say 'No' when you are being pressed from every side to give in to a temptation. That's just a fact of life when you're empowered by the Holy Spirit. There's no excuse, fellas. There's always an exit door. It's just up to us whether we use it or not.

Those of us who have yielded ourselves to Jesus and are living resurrection-lives are no longer slaves to forces that drive us. It doesn't mean we won't feel the pressure to give in, but it does mean that we can stand firm. I remember listening to a mate tell me how he fought off a serious temptation to access some porn online. He told me it was so powerful that all he could do was pray that someone would disturb him. At that moment, his mobile phone went off. It was one of his kids calling him. Saved by the bell!

So, you see, there's always an exit door. We're no longer slaves to sin but pilgrim men who will one day be reunited in resurrection with Jesus. Game on.

---

**Prayer: When You provide me with an exit door, give me the grit and the guts to use it and fight back. Thank You that I am a slave not to sin but to Jesus. Amen.**

---

# 32/Dead or alive ...

'The wages of sin is death, but the gift of God is eternal life in Christ Jesus our Lord.' **Romans 6:23**

On 1 May 1945, Josef Goebbels and his wife, Magda, gave their six children an injection of morphine and then cracked cyanide capsules in their mouths. Shortly after, dressed in full uniform, Goebbels shot his wife and then shot himself. By contrast, in the Warsaw Ghetto, where 300,000 out of 400,000 people were eventually to lose their lives, Jews set up schools, founded an orchestra and carried on making art. Women even had babies!

What made the difference? Simply this: the Jews in Warsaw had an anchor for their souls and had their hope in God. Every day, they said the *Shema* twice, just as previous generations had done for centuries. It comes from Deuteronomy 6:4: 'Hear, O Israel: the LORD our God, the LORD is one.' Hope was part of these people's story. They followed a God who had led their ancestors out of Egypt and parted the Red Sea. That was the definitive difference. In fact, wherever God's heroes have overcome, it has been with a profound sense of God being with them – whether it's Joshua crossing the Jordan or Nehemiah rebuilding the walls of Jerusalem.

The Bible is, as ever, startlingly clear: the wages of sin is death but the gift of God is eternal life. Remember today that you have an anchor for your soul and keep living in the hope and expectation that that gives you. No matter what.

---

**Prayer: Thank You, God, for the hope You give us. Thank You for the gift of Jesus and the fact that I can live a life of optimism and expectation. Amen.**

---

# 33/Watch your step!

'Blessed is the man who does not walk in the counsel of the wicked or stand in the way of sinners or sit in the seat of mockers. But his delight is in the law of the LORD, and on his law he meditates day and night.' **Psalm 1:1-2**

When I was growing up, there were a couple of guys in my town who really stood out. They were bright, talented, switched on and funny and could have had the world at their feet. One of them was a stunning artist and the other, a very gifted musician. Both of them were also in the top group for maths and good at sport as well. Then they took a wrong path. Not together, but a wrong path nonetheless. To this day, neither of them has fulfilled his potential – quite the opposite. In fact, one of them is sadly already dead.

Something similar could happen to any of us at any time. There's a story told of a bishop who was visiting a shelter for the homeless. One of the men he was introduced to looked very familiar. He asked if they had met before, and got the reply: 'I used to be one of your vicars.' It turned out that alcohol and chasing the ladies had taken him down a path he really didn't want to go down.

And there you have it, really. Your sin will take you to places you really don't want to go. It's best to get serious about staying on the straight and narrow. As the psalm says: Don't hang out with the wicked! Stay in the Word, fill your soul with good things, delight in God …

---

**Prayer: Make my crooked steps straight and keep me on the straight and narrow. Don't let me take paths that lead to dead ends but help me to keep walking towards the light of Jesus. Amen.**

---

# 34/Planted

'He is like a tree planted by streams of water, which yields its fruit in season and whose leaf does not wither. Whatever he does prospers.'
**Psalm 1:3**

I'm a man of many interests and one of the diverse things I enjoy is trees. I'm not sure why, I just like them. A particular interest is bonsai trees – mini-trees to the layman – and over the years I've tried to grow my own. Basically, you plant some conkers, grow them for a bit and then gradually transfer them into smaller and smaller pots. One of mine was very successful and looked amazing until it was accidentally thrown away when we were moving house. More bombed than bonsai'd in that case!

You have to feed and water them regularly. In fact, if you don't water them daily, they die very quickly. It's better to be a tree with deep roots, I guess. That's the analogy used here, not of a bonsai but of a proper, full-on tree. Going back to yesterday's notes, if you don't walk with God and you don't meditate on His Word, you'll be starving yourself. The man who does do these things, however, is like a well-planted tree fed by a stream. Roots go deep in trees (unless it's a bonsai). It's deep roots that keep a mighty oak steady against a storm or whatever is thrown at it – but those roots need water or even an oak will come to nothing.

As ever, I guess it's up to us: we either get on with it or we don't. For the man who takes note, though, there is blessing. Why not put the Bible on your phone, Kindle and/or laptop? Why not write some verses and stick them in places where you'll see them? It will make a difference.

**Prayer: I will meditate on your Word, God, and I will do stuff that pleases You. May I be a man whose roots go deep! Show me what I need to do to be such a man. Amen.**

# 35/Watched

'For the LORD watches over the way of the righteous, but the way of the wicked will perish.' **Psalm 1:6**

You often hear someone remarking that they 'have an audience of one'. People say this when they feel they need to say or do something that is right before God but is not going to be popular with anyone else. It's helpful to keep that perspective. What we often don't appreciate, perhaps, is that really God is watching over us all the time. He sees what we are doing even when the door is closed and no one else can look in. Now, for the bloke with a clean conscience, that's pretty cool. Taking it a step further, what the verse is saying is that you're not just being watched but guided – and even, at times, guarded. The Lord is 'watching over your way'.

However, for the bloke who's got something to hide, that becomes a bit of a nightmare, because this verse implies that God will allow you to take a divergent path if you want to – even if in the end it takes you to hell! It's a salutary warning to us guys. How about this as a remedy? Make it your habit each day as you walk out the front door, or settle behind your desk or sit down for your first cuppa, simply to say to God: 'Watch over me today!' I reckon He will answer that prayer and it will give you a sense that heaven is on your shoulder.

---

**Prayer: Watch over my steps and keep me on the narrow path. Guard me from going down a road that will end up doing me in. Lead me in the way everlasting. Amen.**

---

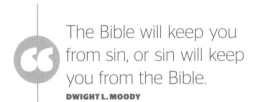

The Bible will keep you from sin, or sin will keep you from the Bible.
**DWIGHT L. MOODY**

## 36/The ego has landed

'All this happened to King Nebuchadnezzar. Twelve months later, as the king was walking on the roof of the royal palace of Babylon, he said, "Is not this the great Babylon I have built as the royal residence, by my mighty power and for the glory of my majesty?"' **Daniel 4:28-30**

A classic 'man fail'. I can remember the line (along with loads of others, if I'm honest) from *Top Gun* when Maverick's boss calls him and Goose in for a roasting after a bit of a close call: 'Your ego's writing cheques your body can't cash. You don't own that plane, the taxpayers do!' That's the trap Nebuchadnezzar was about to fall into. It's easily done. You look at your home, or your kids or your work or whatever, and you give yourself all the credit. You may not be as blatant as him, but deep in the recesses of your heart you pat yourself on the back for a job well done.

Nothing wrong with that, of course, as long as you give the glory and thanks to God.

I guess for me it's all about 'sovereignty'. Do we really grasp that in reality – if God is God, as we believe – our lives are sustained moment by moment, nanosecond by nanosecond, by His grace? If He wanted to turn the lights off, He could. Fact. He can do whatever He wants within His own character (He can't lie, for example). Sometimes we would do well to remember that. Knowing that and understanding the implications keep a man's ego firmly in check.

As I said, there's nothing wrong with feeling good about life or proud of your kids or a job well done. Just be sure to keep the glory for God. It's worth repeating: if people see anything good in you, tell them it's because of the One who is greater than you.

---

**Prayer: Protect me from my ego. Guard me from taking the glory away from You and heaping praise on myself. Help me never to forget Your grace and mercy. Amen.**

---

# 37/Wild thing

'The words were still on his lips when a voice came from heaven, "This is what is decreed for you, King Nebuchadnezzar: Your royal authority has been taken from you. You will be driven away from people and will live with the wild animals; you will eat grass like cattle. Seven times will pass by for you until you acknowledge that the Most High is sovereign over the kingdoms of men and gives them to anyone he wishes."' **Daniel 4:31-32**

I thank God that He is a God of grace and is patient with us. The reality is that if He wasn't, we would generally be in a whole heap of trouble. Sometimes, however, He does take action in order to put us right. It has often been said that it's better to face getting sorted out in this life than in the next. In the case of good old Neb, he was about to be laid low in an epic way. Sure, he was restored later; but for that to happen and for him to be a great king over his people he needed to get his ego in check.

I think there's a warning here for us. Yes, I know that God is gracious and yes, I know He is a God of love and we are post cross and resurrection; but He isn't averse to taking corrective action if necessary. So, how do we respond? Quite simply, I think we need to keep a serious check on our egos. Who do we give the credit to when things go well? Who are we pointing to? Ourselves or others or God? Do we have people around us who will be honest with us and help us sort our heads out when needed? Good questions to ponder on in the light of the lesson we learn from Nebuchadnezzar.

---

**Prayer: Keep my ego in check.
Teach me in this life, God,
how to walk humbly and
graciously before You. Amen.**

---

## 38/True luuurve

'Husbands, love your wives, just as Christ loved the church and gave himself up for her.' **Ephesians 5:25**

Bear with me if you aren't married. You may be one day – and in any event these principles will be helpful as you walk in relationship with others.

So, how *did* Christ love the Church? He died for her, that's how. Next question, then: What does that mean for me if I'm married? Basically, it means that you take the hit, carry the can and make sure that you are the one who apologises first. Forget for a moment all the arguments raging about who is head of the household – they stop us getting to the heart of the matter. Our job is to lead a sacrificial life of love for our family's sake.

It's so powerful when us men do that. I remember once feeling the need to apologise over a row Karen and I had got into many years previously. When I got home, I asked her to forgive me. Note, I didn't say: 'I'm sorry ...' I put the power in her hands. It was quite a moment when I realised that she was still carrying a hurt from all that time ago and it really helped both her and me. Did I find it difficult? Sure did. Did my pride nearly get in the way? Sure did. But that's the point: our job is to lay our lives down. No one said it was going to be easy.

---

**Prayer:** *[If you are married:]* **Help me to love my wife as Christ loved the Church.** *[If you are not:]* **Help me to learn what sacrifice really means so that I will be the man You need me to be in all my relationships. Amen.**

---

# 39/Who cares?

'In this same way, husbands ought to love their wives as their own bodies. He who loves his wife loves himself. After all, no-one ever hated his own body, but he feeds and cares for it ...' **Ephesians 5:28-29**

OK, I know that some people do say that they hate their bodies, but there's a principle here that Paul is trying to establish. Obviously, times were different when he wrote this and blokes would seriously mistreat the women in what was then a very patriarchal society. Things are different now. Or are they?

Are you as attentive to your wife as you are to yourself? If you're not married, what about your girlfriend, or your close friends or members of your family? Who do you put first, yourself or others? Are you known as someone who is caring and kind or selfish and indifferent? Do you go the extra mile for those who are close to you or do you pull back, reluctant to pay the extra cost? Do you share the load at home or do you put your feet up, allowing someone else to do the domestic stuff because 'you've been hard at work'?

These are just some thoughts to get us thinking. If we truly love those around us, we will look after them and make sure they are fulfilled, rested and cared for, every bit as much as we want to be.

---

**Prayer: Help me to be kind, attentive, caring and sacrificial. Help me to look after the interests of others and not just my own. Amen.**

---

Sure, I have friends, plenty of friends, and they all come around wantin' to borrow money. I've always been generous with my friends and family, with money, but selfish with the important stuff like love.

**RICHARD PRYOR**

# 40/Honouring parents

> 'Children, obey your parents in the Lord, for this is right. "Honour your father and mother" – which is the first commandment with a promise.' **Ephesians 6:1-2**

We'll talk about raising kids some other time. For now, I think it's good for us guys to ponder what it means to honour our parents. I know there will be some men out there who have lost their parents, but you will know other blokes who need to sort out how they interact with their parents and perhaps you could help them.

It's fair to say that sooner or later we all exasperate each other. If you're in a relationship for any length of time, the other person will eventually get on your nerves. Your relationships with your mum and dad are no exception. So, how do you 'honour' them? Perhaps you need to cut them some slack. Perhaps you should hear them out when you think you know all the answers. Maybe you need to make the effort to see them more often, to invest more time in their lives. Over the last few years, my dad and I have tried to bag a few trips together. We've gone big game fishing, spent a few days on the Continent here and there and basically 'done life' together. It's good for the soul and good for the memory bank. We only get one shot at life and there's no rehearsal time, so make it count!

As an aside, perhaps if your dad is no longer alive you might consider how you could be a spiritual father to some young guy out there who could use the input. It would give both him and you the chance to be blessed.

As for the promise attached to this commandment, it is that you will lead a long life. So, if you want to collect your pension one day, take note!

---

**Prayer: Help me to be a better son. Help me to be patient and slow to anger. As I honour You as my heavenly Father, so I will try to honour my earthly parents. Amen.**

---

# 41/Mustn't grumble!

'Do everything without complaining or arguing, so that you may become blameless and pure, children of God without fault in a crooked and depraved generation.'
**Philippians 2:14-15**

The language of the street is complaint. Stand in any queue anywhere and listen to how people are talking. Most of the time, I guarantee you, they'll be whingeing and moaning. The newspapers are the same, and so (I'm told) are the soap operas. We live in a society that seems to echo with the sounds of complaint.

As followers of Jesus, we're called to live a different way. So, how about trying to make sure that we always give others the benefit of the doubt? How about trying to believe the best, not the worst, in any given situation? How about getting a reputation as blokes who have only good things to say? How about being known as guys who, even when bad news or negative feedback has to be delivered, deliver it in such a way that it builds people up?

I reckon that men who know they're redeemed and saved have no excuse but to live that way. And one thing I do know is this: we will really stand out! So, let's go for this! Start to exercise some discipline over your thoughts and your tongue. Start to speak in a language that's upbeat rather than negative. Start to kill off an attitude that's more cynical than optimistic.

---

**Prayer: Guard me from being part of the moaning masses! Help me to be a positive influence on those around me. Keep my tongue from complaint and may I say only what is helpful and encouraging from now on. Amen.**

---

# 42/All about me?

'Do nothing out of selfish ambition or vain conceit, but in humility consider others better than yourselves. Each of you should look not only to your own interests, but also to the interests of others.'
**Philippians 2:3-4**

Our motivation for doing stuff is often complex. When I was part of a local church in Essex, I had to pop in to the building one day in the middle of the week to pick something up. As I pulled in round the back, a guy who had mild learning difficulties was there, cutting the hedges that went all the way round the church. To be honest, it had never occurred to me to wonder why they always looked so nice and trim. Now I knew. I asked this guy how often he did this job and he told me he'd been doing it regularly for years. Asking around, it seemed that no one had a clue he'd been doing it. Apparently, everyone just took the nicely trimmed hedges for granted. Interesting, that. If I'd been him, I would probably have dropped a few hints so that I could get some kudos points.

It's a good question to ask ourselves: Why do we do certain things? Is it all about us and getting some applause, or is our motivation purely to serve? Do we just want to look good in front of other people or are we happy for other people to get some glory? A leader may well be tempted to walk past something he built and say, 'Look what I did!' A great leader – a servant leader – walks past and says: 'It's wonderful to have been part of that once. They're doing such great things!'

---

**Prayer: Heavenly Father, help me to do stuff for the right reasons. Test my heart and search my motivation. Pull me up when it's more about me than it should be. Amen.**

---

# 43/United we stand

'If you have any encouragement from being united with Christ, if any comfort from his love, if any fellowship with the Spirit, if any tenderness and compassion, then make my joy complete by being like-minded, having the same love, being one in spirit and purpose.'
**Philippians 2:1-2**

I've been leading teams of people for years now. Being in a team is fraught with challenges. We all come to the party with different character traits and gifts. Some of us are detail people, others are big picture. Some people are annoyingly happy all the time, others get moody. Some people are extroverts, others are introverts. I could go on.

What I've noticed, however, is that the best teams are those that pull together for a common purpose. Generally, they are able to look past the differences amongst themselves and the constant potential for conflict. The worst teams contain people who think it's all about them personally. You know the sort of people I mean: they're the equivalent of the ultra-selfish striker in a football team. Here's the rub. As followers of Jesus, we are called to be one in spirit and purpose. We aren't meant to be embarking on a solo journey but pulling together to see God's kingdom come.

That's a big challenge for blokes, who generally think they know best about everything! But see yourself as part of a squad of men who are here to make Jesus known. Unite around that goal and aim to go and do stuff together.

As an aside, it would seem that that attitude makes God happy ...

---

**Prayer: Help me to be a man who is a good and effective team-player. Help me to look past disagreements and personality differences so that I can see Your kingdom come. Amen.**

---

# [CHOOSE LIFE!]

## 44/ Letting go

'The Advocate, the Holy Spirit, whom the Father will send in my name, will teach you all things and will remind you of everything I have said to you. Peace I leave with you; my peace I give you. I do not give to you as the world gives. Do not let your hearts be troubled and do not be afraid.' **John 14:26-27**

Have you ever heard someone say, 'I don't do change'? During our lifetimes, all of us experience massive amounts of change – a change of job, moving house, the loss of a friend ... Change can leave us feeling low, out of sorts or just plain scared. The disciples must have felt this when Jesus told them that He was leaving: their closest Friend, their Leader, the man they'd left their jobs, homes and ways of life to follow. And yet He offers them just what they need: the Holy Spirit and a sense of peace that the world cannot give.

Change often requires letting go of stuff. We need to be real with ourselves and God about what we are going through, what we are holding on to and what we need to let go of. Change can also mean adapting, figuring out how to do things in a new environment. The disciples had to learn to do life without their Guide, without their Friend. But Jesus does not leave them without help: He leaves them the Holy Spirit to teach them and remind them.

---

**Prayer: Lord God, when change comes, help me to know that You are with me through it all. When I need to let go of things, help me to take up what You offer. Most of all, I ask that You would give me Your peace which is beyond understanding. Amen.**

---

# 45/ Dead or alive?

'... Jesus was troubled in spirit and testified, "Very truly I tell you, one of you is going to betray me. ... It is the one to whom I will give this piece of bread when I have dipped it in the dish." Then, dipping the piece of bread, he gave it to Judas, the son of Simon Iscariot.' **John 13:21,26**

There must have been a time when Judas followed Jesus, when he was His friend. We don't know how close he was to Jesus, but we do know that there was a point when he chose to turn his back on Him and sell Him out. Jesus was not surprised that Judas was ready to betray Him. He knew it was coming. He knew it had to happen. He even says to him, 'What you are about to do, do it quickly.' However, we also see Jesus react in a different way. The Greek word John uses to tell us that Jesus was troubled is the same word he uses to describe Jesus' state when His friend Lazarus died. It suggests a stomach-churning feeling of anguish, of being screwed up inside.

Despite His conflicting emotions, Jesus' love for Judas continues. Dipping bread in a dish of tasty sauce was an Eastern custom that signified friendship. It appears that even when He is faced with His betrayer, Jesus cannot help but show grace.

Are there times when we betray Jesus? Are there times when we turn our backs on Him? Whatever you have done, however you are feeling, Jesus' grace is offered to you. Do we want to be like Judas, going our own way, denying life – or do we want to be like Lazarus: brought back to life by the grace of Christ?

**Prayer: Jesus, help me to recognise my betrayals, help me to see the things that cause You pain. By Your grace and power, lead me into a life worth living. Amen.**

# 46/Prayer and praise

'Is anyone among you in trouble?
Let them pray. Is anyone happy?
Let them sing songs of praise.'
**James 5:13**

I love the way James puts things – it sounds
so matter of fact, so belt-and-braces! In
trouble? Pray. Feeling happy? Praise. It makes
sense, doesn't it? It sounds so simple – but how
often do we do it?

Trouble can take many forms, but let's not forget
that God knows us inside out and He understands
what we are going through better than we do.
Like the song says, 'Nobody knows the troubles
I've seen, nobody knows but Jesus.' Prayer is not
just passing on information, though, it's about
being honest with God and listening and waiting
for His response.

Happiness, too, can take many forms. It could be
a sense of achievement over a job well done, it
could be sharing a moment with someone you

love, or it could even be enjoying a plate of your favourite food! We must not forget to give praise to God for the good stuff as well as being honest about the bad.

God wants us to acknowledge Him at all times, happy or sad, winning or losing, up or down. Prayer and praise are about walking with God through it all. So, if something happens today that throws a spanner in the works, talk to God about it – or if something happens that is good, thank Him!

---

**Prayer: Father, help me to acknowledge You at all times. Help me to be real with You today, through the good stuff and the bad. Amen.**

---

# 47/Don't worry, be happy?

'Therefore I tell you, do not worry about your life, what you will eat or drink; or about your body, what you will wear. Is not life more than food, and the body more than clothes?'
**Matthew 6:25**

These days we are being shouted at from every angle. 'Eat a Yorkie and you'll be a real man, use this deodorant and you'll be irresistible to women, get the best rate on your mortgage, compare car insurance ...' – the list seems endless. And yet Jesus' instruction has the potential to be liberating: Don't worry about your life!

Jesus isn't telling us to become naturists on a diet, He's pointing us to what is important: life. More to the point, life with Him at the centre. When everything around us is telling us what we ought to be concerned about, what we require to be happy, it's important to remember that life is more important than some of the stuff we fill it with.

Today, how about asking God to show you the things He wants you to crack on with, the things He wants you to fill your life with: prayer, honest relationships, fun, joy, laughter ...? How about asking Him to help you to stop worrying about the things you can't control and take control of the things you can in His strength? Try using this prayer of St Patrick:

*I bind unto myself today*
*The power of God to hold and lead,*
*His eye to watch, His might to stay,*
*His ear to hearken to my need;*
*The wisdom of my God to teach,*
*His hand to guide, His shield to ward;*
*The word of God to give me speech,*
*His heavenly host to be my guard.*

---

**Prayer: Lord, help me not to worry. Help me to bring my life issues to you in prayer. Help me to see things from Your perspective, even if I find it difficult. Amen.**

---

## 48/Fruity

'No good tree bears bad fruit, nor does a bad tree bear good fruit. Each tree is recognised by its own fruit.' **Luke 6:43-44**

Jesus goes on in verse 45 to imply that it's all about the state of your heart. Good things, He says, come out of the good that's stored there. I guess for us men it means that, over time, the way you choose to live your life will have an effect on you. Pretty straightforward, really. Do good stuff and your attitude and 'heart condition' will follow – and you'll be all the happier for it.

So, what is this good stuff? A kind word to someone in the office. Making the teas and coffees for everyone. Going the extra mile for someone. Doing something for someone that won't get you anything in return. Being generous, gracious and encouraging. How about losing an argument from time to time? Cheering someone on who you would normally envy or see as a rival or a threat? All these things and more will, over time, change the orientation of your heart.

The interesting thing is that verse 44 says that a tree is recognised by its fruit. That surely means that people will see in you something that's different. When I first came across followers of Jesus, over 22 years ago, I could see they were very different from me. They had an attitude and a peace about them I had never seen before. It drew me to them, and ultimately to Jesus. People see good fruit and it makes a big impression.

Worth a ponder.

---

**Prayer: May my life reflect the character of Jesus and not the world. May people see in me good things that speak of the kingdom. May my life and conduct be a witness to Jesus, wherever I am. If they're not, then stop me in my tracks! Amen.**

---

# 49/Mouthy

'For the mouth speaks what the heart is full of.' **Luke 6:45b**

You meet some people and they are just full of encouragement. Hang around them and you feel 10 feet tall! These sort of people are trustworthy, too. I say that because it's easy to have confidence in people who you never hear say anything bad about anyone. You can be pretty sure that they won't be saying negative stuff about you when you're not around. It's true, isn't it? When some bloke comes up to me and says, 'Did you hear about so-and-so? Just between you and me ...', I just think: 'H'mm! I'd better be a bit careful around you. Who knows what you will say about me some time?'

It's not just that, though, is it? It's an indication of where that person's heart is at. Whatever is in your heart comes out of your mouth. So, here's a thought for today. If you find, when you think about it, that you tend to come out with negative stuff, or you're a bit of a gossip or a whinger, then do the following: shut your mouth. Then keep it shut until you've done some work on your heart.

Believe me, you'll be doing yourself and those around you a real favour. So, ask God to keep your heart right and determine to keep it that way!

---

**Prayer: As I guard my heart and keep it right, let my words be only those that encourage others and build them up. And when I fail to keep it that way, prompt me to put a sock in it and get myself sorted out. Amen.**

---

50/Flaky

'Why do you call me, "Lord, Lord," and do not do what I say?' **Luke 6:46**

I reckon a lot of us men are more like God-fearers, really, than followers of Jesus. What I mean is that we kind of keep God in our back pockets as a sort of insurance policy. Something goes wrong at work and we pray. Something happens at home and we pray. We get ill and we pray. Things are going well for a while – we forget to pray. Then there's the everyday stuff. We go to church and we sing and say prayers; we go to work and somehow we're not quite the same. It can be even worse when we get on the football pitch, where we can bear very little resemblance to the men people know on Sunday.

Walking with Jesus is all about being consistent. It's about being the same man wherever you are, including when no one's looking. Here's a cool challenge: Why not go through some of the Gospels and list half a dozen character traits of people who follow Jesus, and then try and live them out?

Even more scary would be to get someone close to you to tell you honestly how you measure up against some of those traits. We often think we are someone we're not, and that's where the inconsistency comes in. I was talking to someone a few months ago about being kind and I was a bit taken aback when they told me I wasn't seen as being overflowing with kindness myself! It was a fair cop – they named a few people we both know who *are* kind, and compared with them I am not. Since then, I've tried to do something about it. It's not that I'm nasty, more that my inner kindness has been staying, well, 'inner'. It's good to have an audit sometimes!

_____

**Prayer: Quite simply, let my words and actions match up. Help me to be consistent, someone who not only says he's a Christian but lives it as well. Send Your Spirit to help me. Amen.**

_____

# 51/Proper job

'As for everyone who comes to me and hears my words and puts them into practice, I will show you what they are like. They are like a man building a house, who dug down deep and laid the foundation on rock. When a flood came, the torrent struck that house but could not shake it, because it was well built.' **Luke 6:47-48**

Where we used to live in Somerset, there was an expression for when a task had been done well: 'proper job'. In fact, there was a chain of hardware shops called that. I love places like that where you can get practically anything you need. I went into one in search of a very obscure electrical component I needed to finish a job. A bloke in a tan overall, like something out of a *Two Ronnies* sketch, looked at me over his glasses and then opened a drawer and a box inside it, another box inside that and another box inside that one – and there was the very thing I needed. Priceless. A proper shop doing a proper job with no corners cut.

The fact is, if you want to do a proper job you can't cut corners or you'll come unstuck in the end. My shopping experience comes to mind when I read these verses. A proper job in Jesus' view is to do what He has asked of you. The end result is who you become a bloke with deep foundations that won't fall apart when the ground starts shifting or the floods come. Jesus is the rock, and our job is to build our lives on Him. We do that by doing what He says. If we choose to do things our way instead, we'd better cling on hard when things start to get swept away around us.

Perhaps later, reread the Beatitudes (see Days 14–23) and keep challenging yourself.

---

**Prayer: I don't want to be a lightweight, so show me what I need to do to strengthen the foundations of my life and stay rock solid in You. Amen.**

---

# 52/Half a job

'But the one who hears my words and does not put them into practice is like a man who built a house on the ground without a foundation. The moment the torrent struck that house, it collapsed and its destruction was complete.' **Luke 6:49**

In kingdom terms, it seems there's no such thing as half a job. When it comes to following Jesus, you just can't cut corners. When I built a chicken coop recently, I found I paid a price for not concreting in the posts and relying instead on some fence-post spikes. The end result was a wonky coop – not a good look, and not a wife-pleaser. Basically, I had to go out and do it again properly.

It's the same with being a disciple, except that if we don't do it properly we don't end up being a bit lop-sided, we end up getting done over. I've seen it loads of times. You see a fella who has based his walk of faith on his experiences instead of the Word of God and he gets undone the moment the pressure is on. What is more, if you haven't been doing what Jesus asks of you and you've merely been talking about it and being a bit half-cocked, there's no relationship there to lean on in the tough times.

Let's face it, we don't want to end up on the casualty list, so we need to do some work. It's really important to recover the disciplines that build deep foundations: regular Bible-reading, being grace-filled, practising humility and forgiveness, staying faithful – and more besides. Otherwise, you'll be like a boxer going in to face the world champ when all you've done to get fit is walk the dog. When the blows come, you'll last 10 seconds if you're lucky. So, get training and get those foundations built!

---

**Prayer: I resolve to practise spiritual discipline and make my life's foundations strong. Keep me vigilant, Holy Spirit. Amen.**

---

# 53/Aston Martin

'Then he said to them, "Watch out! Be on your guard against all kinds of greed; life does not consist in an abundance of possessions."' **Luke 12:15**

At our recent blokes' camp for hundreds of men around the UK, we managed to arrange for an Aston Martin to be parked in the 'mess tent' so that the guys saw it when they went across after the main meeting. It was an epic moment. The car was brand new and only had the miles on the clock it had taken to get it from Barcelona the previous day. Now, I'm not a total petrolhead but I can admire a thing of beauty like that: a hand-finished, £130,000 supercar. The problem comes when you start to let stuff like that get under your skin and you want a sports car yourself when your budget doesn't quite allow it. In our debt-ridden society, our ability to 'obtain' stuff is off the chart. I get letters nearly every week telling me how big a loan I've been pre-approved for. It's scary.

Jesus warns us about greed and tells us to keep a check on ourselves. Here's my top tip today. If you find that something is getting under your skin and you really want it – a new iPad, perhaps, or a pricey bit of sports kit – my advice is to wait. Give it time and you'll find that very possibly the desire to buy it passes. Of course, if you really need it, that's different. But if it's just that you want it and in all honesty there's a bit of greed at work, or envy of other people who have got it, just park it and see how you feel in a month's time. Most likely, you'll find another, more pressing need for your hard-earned dosh. Like setting up a savings plan for a new Aston Martin. (Joke.)

---

**Prayer: Guard me against greed. Help me not to covet. Help me to be happy with the simple things. Amen.**

---

# 54/Building barns ...

'And he told them this parable: "The ground of a certain rich man yielded an abundant harvest. He thought to himself, 'What shall I do? I have no place to store my crops.' Then he said, 'This is what I'll do. I will tear down my barns and build bigger ones, and there I will store my surplus grain. And I'll say to myself, "You have plenty of grain laid up for many years. Take life easy; eat, drink and be merry."' But God said to him, 'You fool! This very night your life will be demanded from you. Then who will get what you have prepared for yourself?' This is how it will be with whoever stores up things for themselves but is not rich toward God."' Luke 12:16-21

A much longer reading today, but I wanted the parable to speak for itself.

Alexander the Great was 16 when he finished his studies under Aristotle and went to war. He basically lived the rest of his life on campaign and by the time of his death 16 years later he had conquered most of the known world. It's worth reading up on him some time. There's one fascinating thing about him, however, that is rarely mentioned. Despite all his conquests, he asked to be buried in an open casket with his hands spread, to show that he left this world with nothing. Which shows he was quite insightful, because it's true!

It's worth thinking about how we use our money. Why do we store it up? Why do we 'build bigger barns'? Why, as Christians, would we want early retirement? One day, we will stand before God empty-handed and our only asset then will be the way we have lived our lives for Jesus.

---

**Prayer: Show me how You want me to use what You have given me. Inspire me to action and protect me from self-indulgence. Amen.**

---

# 55/ ... and why we do it

'Then Jesus said to his disciples: "Therefore I tell you, do not worry about your life, what you will eat; or about your body, what you will wear. For life is more than food, and the body more than clothes. Consider the ravens: they do not sow or reap, they have no storeroom or barn; yet God feeds them. And how much more valuable you are than birds! Who of you by worrying can add a single hour to your life? Since you cannot do this very little thing, why do you worry about the rest?"' **Luke 12:22-26**

The previous reading leads us on to a tidy thought about worry. The reason we store stuff up is because we worry about the future – will we have enough dosh if the wheels come off for a while? Of course, it's good to be prudent with what we have; we just need to make sure it doesn't become unhealthy. To be blunt, the reason we hoard our money is that ultimately we don't trust God. Suppose you're in church and the offering plate comes around. In your pocket are a fiver and a £20 note. Why do you just put the fiver in? Is it because you're mean? Possibly. Or is it anxiety that is really at the root of it?

In my experience, those who truly trust God are among the most generous people I know. So, challenge yourself. Think about your spending and your saving and ask yourself if you really trust God. Perhaps there is something He has asked you to do but you haven't done it because of the possible financial implications. So much good stuff doesn't happen for that reason. Don't allow yourself to be one of those guys who quit on the shot.

---

**Prayer: Deliver me from unhealthy worrying about money. Help me to know, deep in my heart, that You will watch out for me if I step out for You. Amen.**

---

# 56/Give it all up!

'Do not be afraid, little flock, for your Father has been pleased to give you the kingdom. Sell your possessions and give to the poor. Provide purses for yourselves that will not wear out, a treasure in heaven that will never fail, where no thief comes near and no moth destroys. For where your treasure is, there your heart will be also.'
**Luke 12:32-34**

So, give to the poor, sell your possessions (presumably so you can give away the proceeds) and build up your treasure in heaven. H'mm ... Not many of us doing that, I suspect – which in itself is something worth pondering on. I mean, why don't we live more simply? Why are we so mean? Could we be more generous to those who have, frankly, very little in comparison with us?

There's another juggernaut of a thought in here that is also well worth spending a couple of minutes on today. 'Where your treasure is, there your heart will be also,' says Jesus. Now, that's pretty incisive. I guess that 'kingdom treasure' could be seen as many things. For me, I think my treasure is the people I've seen come to faith in Jesus. It'll be amazing, won't it, when we finally get home and see a few of our mates there and some members of our family. Imagine what it will feel like when they tell us they are there only because we never gave up praying for them or telling them about Jesus. That's real treasure!

Now, if you believe that and live for that, it'll do your heart good – whereas I suspect that if you live for money or the things of this life you will only realise, when you finally look back on your life in the light of Jesus, what a massive distraction they were from what is really important.

---

**Prayer: I determine to be a man whose treasure is heavenly, not worldly. Guard me from being distracted by the latest kit. Help me to keep my focus on what Jesus wants and values. Amen.**

---

# 57/Herrings

'Accept the one whose faith is weak, without quarrelling over disputable matters. One person's faith allows them to eat anything, but another, whose faith is weak, eats only vegetables. The one who eats everything must not treat with contempt the one who does not, and the one who does not eat everything must not judge the one who does, for God has accepted them.' **Romans 14:1-3**

OK, before we start doing a number on vegetarians and some of my lentil-eating mates start throwing a wobbly, let's remember that this was a row over new believers who couldn't let go of some old religious taboos such as not eating pork. It's not vegetarianism that is in Paul's sights here. Being a veggie is fine; what is not fine is saying that everyone who isn't a veggie has got it wrong. Feel free to make a stand on an issue of conscience – just accept that it may not be right for everyone.

However, what Paul is using the whole veggie thing for is to make a point about the stupidity of falling out over things that aren't really crucial to the faith. If it's not an essential, it's a distraction and we should just park it and move on. It's amazing how many churches get slapped in the face by red herrings. I would list the kind of issues I'm thinking of but I fear I would have herrings thrown at me by a lot of people who love to make majors out of minors. Suffice it to say that we really should stop arguing over the coffee in church (unless it really *is* bad!). Let's get concerned about the real deal: loving God, telling people about Jesus and living for the kingdom. The rest is peripheral.

---

**Prayer: Guard me from falling out with people over trivial issues that You aren't really that bothered about. Help me to see things clearly and keep stuff in perspective. The next time there's a stupid row in my church over something of no consequence, use me to bring some clarity! Amen.**

---

# 58/Account

'You, then, why do you judge your brother or sister? Or why do you treat them with contempt? For we will all stand before God's judgment seat. It is written: "As surely as I live,' says the Lord, 'every knee will bow before me; every tongue will acknowledge God.'" So then, each of us will give an account of ourselves to God.' Romans 14:10-12

It's amazing, really, how we can live with so many blind spots. I don't know about you but I tend to be able to see all the faults in everyone else but think I am mostly free of them. Sometimes it's simply hilarious. It's a bit like *The X Factor* when people go in for an audition who are totally convinced that they're the next Engelbert Humperdinck when in fact they sound more like a dying hyena. It comes as such a profound shock when they're told the truth, because in their own heads they're awesome!

We laugh at people like that, or else we feel really sorry for them and wonder how someone could get it so wrong. The problem is that most of us have the same *X Factor* folly thing going on, just in different ways. So, says Romans 14, watch your own life. Stop judging everyone else and look carefully at what you are about. The bottom line is that we will all give an account of our lives to God, so it's better that we see clearly what we are about now, rather than when it's too late to do anything about it.

---

**Prayer: Please eradicate my blind spots. Help me to see in my life what You see. Help me to become a man who is complete in You. Help me also to stop judging others and treating the people I think are inferior to me with contempt. Help me to see that in You all people are equal. Amen.**

---

# 59/You lose

'I am convinced, being fully persuaded in the Lord Jesus, that nothing is unclean in itself. But if anyone regards something as unclean, then for that person it is unclean. If your brother or sister is distressed because of what you eat, you are no longer acting in love. Do not by your eating destroy someone for whom Christ died.'
**Romans 14:14-15**

Sometimes it's just the right thing to concede an argument and not dig your heels in over an issue. Back to the food business. Some people in Paul's day wanted everyone to eat only veggie meals, some people didn't think eating meat was a problem because they were free in Christ. The latter were right but they were also wrong. Our approach should basically be: for the sake of peace, be prepared to lose an argument if it's not that important at the end of the day. If we really loved one another, we'd be willing to do that.

# 60/A final word

'Love must be sincere. Hate what is evil; cling to what is good.' **Romans 12:9**

I'm writing this sitting on the sofa, with my wife, my kids, my dog and my cat around me and a pile of their bits and pieces. I like being with everyone else when I'm writing - usually - but occasionally, like now, it can get right up my nostrils. So, it's appropriate that I had selected this verse for the last thought of *Son/See/Surf*. I must tell myself this more often: cling to what is good!

I like the use of the word 'cling' - it kind of speaks of hanging on in there with all your strength and all your will. I've got an image of Sylvester Stallone in the movie *Cliffhanger*, desperately holding on to someone, with every ounce of strength he has, to stop them falling thousands of feet to their death. Sometimes pursuing the path of what is good is so like that. It would be easy, wouldn't it, to lose your rag and jump off the narrow way of following Jesus and give in to the 'dark side'. Let's not be like that, though.

So, now let's apply that to living life day by day, at work and at home. Do we men really need to win every argument? Do we really need to be vindicated on every finer point of a debate? Does it really matter that much? Of course it doesn't. When we dig our heels in, it's usually because we feel a bit indignant or because of our pride. The bottom line is that it really sucks when we get like that. It causes loads of tension and upsets everyone. Let's man up a bit and be strong by losing every now and again. After all, what's really important is that God knows the truth. And what's even more important than that is that in all these things He sees our hearts.

---

**Prayer: Help me to be a loser sometimes. Help me to see love as the most important thing, rather than winning every point. Amen.**

---